RUMBA ATOP THE STONES

ACKNOWLEDGMENTS

I am grateful to those publications where these poems first appeared, sometimes in earlier forms:

ACM: "Siglo de Oro"; *The Americas Review*: "Agua de Coco," "Isabel Kongo," and "The Tropics Reclaim Calvary"; *The Antioch Review*: "The Music of Lifeless Creatures"; *Apalachee Quarterly*: "Alina"; *Callaloo:* "AfroCuba"; *The Caribbean Writer*: "An Island Called Wewee" and "Piedad and Her Tonsured Seagulls"; *Chelsea*: "Widowers," "Crib of Reeds," and "Sade"; *Crab Orchard Review*: "God's Veins" and "Osaín"; *Indiana Review*: "Fish Heads" and "Doña Flora's Hothouse"; *Many Mountains Moving*: "Women of Guaraguasi"; *Negative Capability*: "The Stonebreaker's Daughter"; *Notre Dame Review*: "Bitter Algae"; *Ploughshares*: "Requiem Shark with Lilies"; *Private*: "Clouds"; *Samizdat*: "Dido's Lament," and "Iroko." Tía Chucha Press published "Fish Heads/Cabezas de Pescado" and "The Stonebreaker's Daughter/La Hija de un Cantero" in *Astillas de Luz/Shards of Light* (Olivia Maciel, editor). Partisan Press will publish "Alina" in *Clockpunchers: Poetry of the American Workplace* (Virgil Suarez and Ryan G. Van Cleave, editors). Story Line Press will publish "Bone and Blood" in *Place of Passage: Catholic Poets Writing about Their Faith* (David Craig and Janet McCann, editors). Some of the poems in this collection also appeared in *Borderlands with Angels*, a winner of the 1994 Bacchae Press Chapbook Contest.

ORLANDO RICARDO MENES

RUMBA ATOP THE STONES

PEEPAL TREE

First published in Great Britain in 2001
Peepal Tree Press Ltd
17 King's Avenue
Leeds LS6 1QS

ISBN 1 900715 49 2

CONTENTS

I. Doña Flora's Hothouse

Doña Flora's Hothouse 11
Widowers 13
The Tropics Reclaim Calvary 15
Fish Heads 17
Clouds 19
Dido's Lament 20
Requiem Shark with Lilies 22
The Music of Lifeless Creatures 24

II. Crib of Reeds

AfroCuba 29
Crib of Reeds 31
Poem Written for the Feast of Our Lady of Charity 33
God's Veins 36
Women of Guaraguasi 38
Alina 41
Isabel Kongo 42
Tropical Christ 44
Osaín 45
Piedad and Her Tonsured Seagulls 47
The Stonebreaker's Daughter 49
Sade 51
Physical Properties of Faith 53
Siglo de Oro 54
Middle Passage 56

III. Caliban Cimarrón

An Island Called Wewee   63
Madrid, 1938   65
Bone and Blood   69
Ironman's Song   71
Agua de Coco   73
Antojitos   75
Iroko   76
Bitter Algae   78
Caliban Cimarrón   81

Notes   83
Glossary   86

for my wife

I. DOÑA FLORA'S HOTHOUSE

DOÑA FLORA'S HOTHOUSE

The Sargasso Sea in cyclone
season, a flotilla of blessèd corpses
drifting in equatorial currents,
their shaved heads crowned with laurel
to repel lightning, sargassum fronds
swathing both neck and limb.

Tiny crabs burrow ears
oozing cerumen, pipefish slither
into sutured wounds that coffer
bones of African St. Barbara.

In the tropics the blessèd are incorruptible,
whether Goa, Malabo, or Hispaniola.
Landfall at Doña Flora's island
(longitude of Gonave and Barbuda),
green thumb hermit who cultivates

their bodies in a hothouse by the sea.
Sheared parts fructify in African soil
from Ilé-Ifé, guano of *Caná-Caná*
vulture that flies to heaven carrying
missives, prayer beads and pits.

Swinging her calabash censer,
Doña Flora fumigates with sarsaparilla
entrails of tamarind, soursop kidneys,
banana toes; a *zunzuncito* hummingbird
flies out her ear to sip balsam tears.

11

Suspended amid laelia orchids
mulatto cherubs trumpet *sones*
from Oriente, Doña Flora rattles

her maraca to sprinkle aguardiente
on guava bladders, uteri of red
papaya, mango hearts. By white

mangroves a shanty of lignum vitae,
dried thatching, barnacled crosses.
All Souls' Day and Doña Flora enters
with her animals, laying overripe fruits

on whitest linen. Iguanas chew
sweet-acid tamarind, a *jutía* rat
nibbles guava, *Caná-Caná* rips papaya –
seeds bursting out – as Doña Flora skins

a mango, bruised with machete,
lifts the bleeding fruit to bands
of amber light, sweet flesh dissolving
in her mouth, its bare stone returned to sea.

WIDOWERS

A raised dance floor, bleached linoleum,
trestlework of crutches, rails strung
with viscera, esophagi (iodine-
tinted streamers), the scent of lysol,
not the sea. Along scabby islands,

keys of convalescence, the widowers
jubilee, dancing with papier-mâché
mannequins that drag rattling dentures,
spill pearly rice, their wives' bridal
portraits glued to their faces.

They – grinning – shake, grind, thrust
rumba yambú to skull maracas,
tibia claves, ribcage guiro; bedpans
bongo to their scuffling beat.

The sun declines before their exhaustion,
the dream collapsing like a paper
boat. The men shrink to their tumors
vegetating in petri dish nurseries
that stink of blood and urine.

A buoy tolls in the swelling tide,
salt-of-silver waves glinting in moonlight;
a woman with Venus' flytrap
eyes, jellyfish skin towers
before them, tentacles with stingers
and feelers mantling her shoulders.

"I'm not here to give hope or sing of life,"
she says. "Think of death, its fragrance
of mangoes rotting, perfume to flies.
A sky of burnt sienna, crosses of carrion

flower and granadilla, death camas;
black nightshade: requiem villanelle.
Dandelions, dandelions ravished
by winds of spring, plumed seeds
drifting and gliding lentissimo."

THE TROPICS RECLAIM CALVARY

Passionflower vines
on banks of Yumurí
three royal palms
crowning a green hill
the middle one
spires into a rainbow

In their allamanda bower
Sts. Lazarus and Barbara
drink rose-apple cider
eat avocado and turtle fricassee
rivulets of passion juice
cascade into gaping seraphim

Toes tapping bongos
Lázaro strums his crutch
with leprous fingers
lamenting his infirmities
"woe begets woe begets woe
I loathe rubbing urine
and tobacco on my boils"

Barbarita replies
warbling a *danzón*
to the sacred heart
"I died for you, no regrets,
mi cielo, mi gloria . . . "
her long cinnamon hair
ablaze with torch lilies

Lázaro feels jealous
toward Jesús – darkly
handsome – whom she's
loved for millennia

Lázaro's bones ache
as never before, wishes he were
an African god – beautiful,
healthy – who drums
the world enrapturing mortals
and immortals alike

FISH HEADS

A glowing crucifix (five
flashing lights) atop the lobster trap,
a rosary of papaya seeds,
a clock like a flaming heart
that shudders every hour;
the heart speaks: "I thirst,
It is finished, etc."

The fisher's son, an acolyte,
sleeps cuddled up in his canoe
of mist, rocking like censer
or bell buoy. Child of the sea,
river, lagoon — Antillean *querubín*,
who drools rose water on the pillow,
commands dolphin and barracuda
to weave arabesques of crown, cross, and pike,
boats skimming with sails of flogged skin.
Inside a pelican's pouch he flies from island
to island, wreathing with rain-lilies
light houses, masts, and campanili.

In their shack of tamarind wood,
a chapel on stilts, the smoke of candles
vivifies fish heads (nailed to the wall)
to bleed, quiver, turn east at cock-crowing;
a procession of ants will then surrender
to the flames. Lye falls
from clouds of ash. Lenten night:
the resurrection ferns will again be lush

and green. Yesterday the sea was vinegary,
less brackish than customary for baptism.
Waves release rosaries gnarled
with bladder wrack that village youths
unravel to mourn another acolyte.
Fragrant as sweet plantain, three mulattas –
fishnet menders – sing a dirge in Lucumí,
pantomime the hammerhead's thrust
and thrash to sign the boy's martyrdom.

Yemayá, Lady of the Sea, spawned
without sin, light from darkest water,
spare the fisher's son, swaddle him with fish
guts, brood him under your manta wings.
That blinding aureole will forever
burn above your shark's-jaw crown.

CLOUDS

To the air clouds are vessels
whose compass marks the instinct of birds,
whose sails aspirate
currents that rudder wildly (mystics'
albatrosses) and billow
like bladders, skirts, or adders
their cold incontinence.
And in pregnant holds raindrops
when unburdened fall
not in hymnal cadences
but like convents' knockers, bricks, and tomes
to slake seas, whose shores crinkle
like Mary's belly after birth.

DIDO'S LAMENT

Habaneros — high and low — have been obsessed
with *la* diva Maria Signorelli
since she arrived from Saint-Domingue
aboard a sloop crammed with French refugees.
Besides the usual *décima* verses,
minuets, and statues of Florentine marble
allegorizing La Siciliana
as Venus de Milo, the Bishop declares
that her voice is identical to Eve's
and should thus be venerated by way
of novenas, although his black
cook Delfina tells everyone at the Market
His Excellency is merely an infatuated
lover. Slaves recently brought from Lagos
swear La Diva is really an *orisha*
having seen her talk to manatees,
take flight with olivaceous cormorants.
Enemies rumor she's not Italian at all
but a quadroon tavernwench from Santiago
who sang salacious guarachas for pieces of eight.
Her décolleté and extravagant
coquetries scandalize *les grand dames*
who call her Whore of Babylon, which makes her laugh;
dangerous Jacobin for giving alms
of emerald and allowing her Haitian seamstress
Cécile to stroll alongside, arms entwined.

Blacks and poor whites — a few aristocrats
in disguise — gather at Cathedral Square
to watch La Venus Siciliana float on gold-
thread Turkish sandals; a threadbare *guajirito* —

country boy – darts toward her touching the train
of an exquisite muslin dress; she takes out
marzipan todies from hair coifed with meringue
rosebuds, hurling the birds with flourish,
sings Dido's Lament *in bravura* –
ascending to four-line C. Frenzied men and women
breach the civil guards' line of bayonets,
crush her lungs as they strip hair, clothes to sell or keep
for scapulars. La Habana mourns in round-the-clock
corteges, the Bishop sermonizes
for sainthood, her house on Aguacate Street
a temple for pilgrims whose lights,
boatswains affirm, can be seen from two leagues away.

REQUIEM SHARK WITH LILIES

Sailor boy in pantaloons guides his jacaranda
caravel through a labyrinth
of skulls, lichens bleeding in fontanels,
Easter winds
spraying heliotropes with ammonia.
Another makes a halo
stirring sand in brine that has preserved
a martyr's spleen 1,000 years.

St. Agnes sweeps the beach with coco fronds
collecting crossfish,
aureole urchins, angels' quills.
Jumps over a small requiem shark
half buried in wet sand:
its transparent body barbed with diamonds,
ten lilies suspended inside a glass

womb. Breaking the membrane with a weathered
pelican's beak, she tingles
as formaldehyde spills
down to her calcareous toes. One flower
begins to dig a burrow,

flailing iridescent petals very fast.
St. Agnes snatches the lily,
putting it in her clenched hand, which secretes
burning nectar through
the pistil; two stamens — long, spiculed —
squeeze her ring finger until it's blue.

She shakes her hand furiously,
its grip becomes tighter, the horny-beaked
stigma punctures
her fingertip, implants black ovules
that mix with her own blood
as it shoots over breakers. Gust shatters the arc,

the lily dies; rainbow droplets coagulate
coating seeds that germinate
inside fish bellies, alive in purgatory's trenches,
then migrate home with their hosts
at the start of Lent and breed on Easter Sunday.

THE MUSIC OF LIFELESS CREATURES

in memory of Amando Fernández (1949-1994)

Indeed, Trinculo was an ass — *culo* means just that —
whelped at Sardinia in a trough of onions
and dungy groats, mother a dregs-pickled
donkeymonger's wench from Galicia,
went penniless by pilgrim's road
to mother's Vigo, rose to wharfbordello clown
crowned with cockles, regal pizzle in hand.

Ariel, hatred is flatulence to old men.
Smell this sea of our exile, each wave-
slop wind of Trinculo's gutbellows.
Decades ago Prospero abandoned
us on this iguana coast; "Imprison me
in cloven pine" you begged, his caduceus
made you mortal with splayfoot, tin ear.

Miranda's blue-green eyes were my sea
and firmament; I gathered moon jellies,
sea nettles, Portuguese men-of-war
to grace her bedpost or footpath,
watched swallows in the hundreds
build mud nests on the rocky cliffs,
their music silenced adders in my ears.

Miranda, my queen angelfish
hiding in coral thicket I easily stunned
with crushed *tagua* seeds, grasped the numb beauty
with my claws, bit her head like custard
apple, savoring the juices. Osprey,
hawk, or eagle could not prey better.

After a summer downpour, earth smelling
of tobacco, my groin rubbed
with fishblood, I hid behind a cycad
to hear Miranda sing, jugging rainwater
under a tamarind tree. Mother warned
against desire, "Gaze at the sea
by moonlight, loneliest of mirrors,
and you will sigh." I wasn't happy in youth,

unlike you who continue being vain,
that silly seawig of turtle grass you put on
in dawn's scatlight, the vineskirt of corallita,
the fisheye baubles round your wrinkled
neck, prattling and prancing as a naiad
to naked fisherboys. Or wearing a wreath

of frangipani, you – who were Prospero's hurdy
gurdy monkey – attempt to charm a sponge husk,
bullcricket, *caimán*, ladies-of-the-night
dully reciting dull sonnets on cloud-
water, seawater, coconutwater, bladderwater, etc.

For you exile's been difficult,
mortality even worse. Submit and learn,
there's wisdom, power in decay. The mysteries
of verse are found in music of lifeless creatures,
listen to a dolphin's innards, the raveled skull
of a castaway, the urn in a *caracol*.

II. CRIB OF REEDS

AFROCUBA

Mi patria es dulce por fuera, / y muy amarga por dentro
Nicolás Guillén

Thirteen years I've been loading sacks of sugar
onto freightships bound for New York and Louisiana,
at times praying they sink so the lumps
will dissolve like a white ghost. Sugar *is* the black
man's curse. I'm a hammer-and-machete
Marxist-Leninist revolutionary
tropical-star Soviet grandson-of-maroon
Stalinist *cabrón*. The Bourgeoisie's destruction
will happen sooner than anyone thinks,
every sugar mill bombed to the ground, the richest land
in America collectivized for indigenous
agriculture. During the Depression,
the cane harvest – *la zafra* – was just 62 days long,
with papá employed the rest of the year playing dominoes,
drinking rum, screwing sugar-mill whores
on credit, died at 42 from cirrhosis of the liver.
As a maid, mamá earned enough to buy cracklings
she cooked with yuca and malanga; we gorged
on spoiled bananas and mangoes. Compadre,
the runs were a condition of my childhood.
When papá died we stayed with Aunt Marta
in Old Havana, who taught mamá to fix clothes
on a jumpy old Singer, and I began to work at the docks
with Uncle Cuco, a communist. I'll never forget
Albertico – red as a crab – who hung a rope
in our town's dancefloor to separate blacks and whites.
If a light-skinned mulatto pretended to pass, he'd throw stones

29

calling him *negro bembón*, *saco de carbón*
(big-lipped black, sack of coal). His *brujero* uncle
took revenge: hexed with fresh-dug human bones and rooster

gizzards, Albertico lost his cruel voice forever.
I don't believe in the African saints but just in case —
por si las moscas — I give Agayú, patron of dock
workers, each Saturday, sliced apples and *cerveza*.

CRIB OF REEDS

Blood and aguardiente.
Tallow, sweat. Eva Kaplan pushes
and screams, cussing in Yiddish,
her buttocks covered with sores
that never seem to heal. Isaac rumples
his straw hat nervously praying
to Adoshem, eyes stinging from sweat,
feet swollen in the tropical heat.
A young boy – barefoot and ragged –
switches a pig drawn by smells
of birthing. Eva's black midwife,
Ma Josefa, cuts the umbilical cord
with machete, elemental iron,
chanting ancestral praises to Yemayá,
orisha of maternity; altar lights,
sea-blue, tongue the rag-doll goddess,
her fan shell, cowries, salted tobacco.
In her crib of reeds and wild cotton
the newborn breathes air, warm and maternal,
that rises from canefields in the rainy
season. 1918: month of Tevet,
the Kaplans escape pogroms
and Bolsheviks, cursing the cold ground
of their birth. At first Cuba's sun
nauseates Eva, gives Isaac headaches,
both break out with hives eating papaya.
They think the *orishas* are *sotens* –
devils – *tambores* and dancing terrify them,
Eva touches black children's hair
to see if it's real. The Kaplans struggle

31

to learn *bozal* Spanish, tongue of slaves;
home's a dirt-floor hut thatched with guinea grass,
a tin charcoal stove on which to cook
black beans and rice, plantains, sweet potato;
without a *shoykhet* meat is unclean,
though Eva enjoys eating stewed *jutía*,
which she says tastes like hen.
Isaac peddles *shmates* – cheap stockings, ties,
cologne – in Sta. Clara's sugar mills.
On holy days the Kaplans and their neighbors
share stories of Middle Passage horrors,
Red Sea miracles. Children of Olofi
and Elohim, Mackandal and Joshua,
Moses and Orúnmila, Ilé-Ifé and Israel.

POEM WRITTEN FOR THE FEAST
OF OUR LADY OF CHARITY

I climb the 50 steps
to her temple
of sugar bricks
that refract light
into tropical aureoles,
rays of red mutisia,
blue sage, violet ivy,
yellow nosegay, etc.

Her Atrium
of Mysteries
has 3 gates:

1. the one for the dead, which I seal with beeswax & mud of
   Calvary.
2. the one for the living dead, hammer shut with 5 fingerbones
   of St. Roch.
3. the one for the living, enter dancing.

Bow 32 times
at the Portal of Sacrifice.

Her black angel
hands me the sacred knife of Isaac & I slaughter
6 white hens, 1 red capon.

On the sabbath
she will feast on clean meat & blood
fermented with cinnamon.

I crawl through passageways
climb Jacob's ladder – 70 rungs –
enter her Hall of Royal Palms.

Sitting on a throne of braided fronds
La Virgen María – vanilla skin, tresses like
aerial roots of *jagüey* ficus –

makes doves & lambs from Torah parchment,
singing hymns to the sun.

      Archangel Gabriel
      rattles rosary beads

I bring you meat, sweet blood
for fertility & 6 loaves of the sabbath.

The 3 holy jewels
for your Crown of Victory
I will knead
from molten candlewax.

      Gabriel beats goatskin drum of Jericho.
      Two cherubs play *el bongó*.

I rhumba Mogen Davids, Latin crosses
in her honor
(Sanctus Sanctus Sanctus)

      She dances *la* conga on sugar skulls,
      I smell caramel of Shekinah.

La Virgen's face glows white-hot,
glory-lily flames budding from fingertips.

O Merciful María
Bendita tú eres entre todas las mujeres
Love from love:
holy splendor, *luz pura*

"You want to know where God is," she says, "what tongue He speaks, the One who is the word & the absence of the word. His light blinds & you will be like a moth drawn to the lamp. Fall into the abyss of God's love. Be consumed by His dazzling darkness."

Dusk falls, clouds scud
over *la* sierra, thundering rain
      dissolves the temple.

          Sugar water cascades
              down this holy mountain,
                  pouring into Sea of
                    First Tears.

Mary takes my hand.
    We leap into the abyss.

GOD'S VEINS

St. Peter Claver sleeps on nests of great blue heron
                              − fish eggs shimmering
                              in standing holy water −
a smoked sardine tied between
each armpit (*to keep Beelzebub away*) his bed's legs mangrove
        roots that extend

all the way to Aruba; from there capillaries
                    radiate to Curaçao, Bonaire, and all Windward
                              Islands, the most defenseless

against storms: *God's veins* he tells his African
converts *stronger than nkisi* − fetish − *of Noah's cypress ark*
                                        or Eden's kapok,
tree of life St. Peter Claver preaches all over Cartagena
the wheel is Satan's invention: *Only by walking*
                    will we ever enter the New Jerusalem

Hates paper, books, printing press, ink, quills
        works of man, *ungodly things*) his supplications scratched
on leathery pitch-apple leaves that ferment in *chicha*

                    Lent's purple-maize liquor.
Brine rains down Cartagena.
Bells toll Stations of the Cross.
                    Ten Africans, men and women,
all christened George, are brought
in chains
to hear St. Peter Claver's catechism: *Be devout in all things*
                    bathe daily with your own tongues

eat only fish, just the heads
                    drink salt water at morning, especially if ill
Demonstrates how the crucifix has everyday uses: anchor, bow,
            scratcher, digging stick, knocker, hone, hammer
The Africans laugh. *Labour is godly* he scolds
even Christ would hammer his own cross, nail his own hands and feet
                                        with a crucifix
Makes them whistle, a few sound like birds.

        Only a short s separates pecado from pescado – sin from fish –
Don't ever omit that s, hell awaits if you do
Make it very long, sibilant, never hissing, so that you lose your breath
                                        in rapture

WOMEN OF GUARAGUASI

Grotto of coquina
whose glass anchors
glint reef wavelets, noonlit,
seven candles – indigo –
melting into pelican droppings,
avian stalactites. Women

of Guaraguasi – spongers and fishers –
harmonize psalms
that cense Chola Kalunga
with nutmeg, cilantro – strophe, refrain;
vanilla fingers interlace
chained molars – caried and ivory.

Chola Kalunga, dancer of whirlpools,
contralto who augurs
hurricanes – spawned in Gulf of Guinea –
miasma that envelops lovers
arousing rapture, jealous tantrums.
Rosa Alelú prepares the Virgin
for her spring-tide fiesta, rubbing *majá-*
grease on voluptuous hips,
capping ebony toes with gold thimbles.

Paved with coral stars
Guaraguasi empties into a bay
where teredos decompose
a slaver's ribcage and rags of turtle meat –
green *caguama* – cure in continuous
spindrift. Heading the comparsa
is Rosa Alelú – clay mask of grouper –

who gurgles ron añejo,
wiggles an enormous tail at goatboys,
her chihuahuas somersaulting
on tambourine. Shawm, billy-goat drums,
double bell, bagasse confetti,

starfish dust. The dogs shimmy a conga
between the legs of Rosa's daughters, bodies sponged
with cane juice and dorado glitter,
who carry the Virgin in her wicker boat,
cinnamon-masted, five black-eyed pea tamales
rolled into barrels, annatto yellow.

Her vessel tied with green ribbon
to a quebracho phallus – ax-breaking wood –
Rosa genuflects, supplicating Chola
Kalunga to bring back bountiful seasons
when Guaraguasi was not overfished
by giant trawlers, nets killing whole schools

of dolphin. Waves recede and eddy
as equatorial currents reverse
their westerly direction, homeward to Accra
Ouidah, Lagos, Cabinda, Benguela;
its green tether snapped, the wicker boat rolls
beyond sight. Months later, while digging
for leathery *caguama* eggs, Rosa's daughter finds
a pigmy – unconscious, shriveled, gangrenous

from drinking seawater. Revived with mallow tea
she tells Alma her past life as Chola
Kalunga, the perilous return to Africa,
abandoning water as a toad, then as green mamba,

tricking creatures to mate, eating them in turn.
Convinced sex is futile, she forsakes immortality,
assuming a woman's body to preach
celibacy among old votaries. Alma kisses
her cowrie beads, drowns the pigmy in a tidal pool.

ALINA

On a bowed clothesline
cotton shirts shrivel like tobacco leaves,
wind sweeping dry cuffs
on the courtyard floor. Her cast-iron

iron on a horseshoe, bottles of lye, starch,
cologne strung to seven nails; and thrown
into a pail knotted albs to unravel.

Scrubbing drill linen on a washboard of oak,
corrugated zinc, Alina's long black hands
scrape *guaguancó*, rumba of barracoons,
rumba to attract Oshún, owner of love

and mountain river, hips and arms
laboring music that slave laundresses,
cane cutters, midwives performed in secret
to gratify gods disguised

as Catholic saints. Like her mother, grandmother,
great-grandmother (enslaved in Calabar),
Alina *lavandera*, the whorls of her thumbs

worn away, burn scars like tobacco leaf.
She'll scrape that guiro, bone-cutting metal,
till calloused knuckles bleed and Oshún

arrives from her sacred forest: a *mayito*
redwing jiggling the clothesline,
dipping into soapy water,
whispering and wheezing metallically.

ISABEL KONGO

Front teeth cut in half-moons
crocodile birthmark
that rubbed with *gua-guao* pepper
wrinkles into Kumbembé
chameleon avatar
of Trickster Nkuyu Nfinda
called Eshu in Yoruba

Left ear chopped off
for running away a second time
Isabel Kongo
kills her Basque overseer
twelve machete slashes
in groin, legs and chest
sixteen tic-tac-toe squares
over solar plexus
Angunga mark for cemetery

Greasy cross on forehead
her limbs roped to pole-chair
El Garrotero tightens
the metal collar like a vise

until Isabel tastes green banana
cooked in ashes
her left fist surrendering
rusty-nail talisman
rolled in African yam leaf

Dies Irae Dies Irae
Isabel Kongo laid
between constricting roots

of ficus Malomuka
Wangara Wangara Simandie

Agnus Dei Agnus Dei
whose blood feeds
cowrie-eyed Nkuyu
three Guinea drums
beating *Foforifó Foforifó*

Malomuka's roots
writhe like twin pythons
Hosanna in excelsis
slowly ingest Isabel
In paradisum Kongo

Pierce my hands and feet
With cloves
Draw henna crosses on my groin
Light candles
Of zebu fat, rosary-wicks
Pour he-goats' wine
Melt the silver candlesticks
Pray to me in ñáñigo
Papimiento, kreole
All hybrid tongues
Set one hundred cane fires
To cense Heaven
The Deed of Redemption
Will be written
On my dark skin
Ink of my Carib blood
Sugar of Paradise
Will burn my lips

OSAÍN

Herbalist and curandero,
cigar maker to *santería* gods, Silvio dries
maduro skins harvested
in darkness – new moon – to prevent holes, blemishes,
any weakening of *ashé* – life force.

                                               Three coronas burn in wood
candlesticks, carved Ibo seraphim;
Silvio pours Haitian cane liquor into sequined shot glasses,
rolls tobacco *cucuruchos* –
cones – stuffing them with possum livers,
                          offerings to Osaín, Patron of curanderos
                          Intercessor who never sleeps
                          keeping vigil over the sick.
This *orisha* sprang
from Africa's humus – no seed, a cutting of God's ulna –
without genitals, other body parts;
taught Adam and Eve
which wild plants were medicinal, which mortal;
preached obedience.
                        Doesn't dance or sing.

The village *framboyán* – Madagascar flame tree –
has bloomed early
presaging death of children; women smear
cocoa butter on the trunk
imploring Osaín to protect their firstborn.

                        Silvio and Tin Tin Tamacún,
his 20-pound calico,
prowl the canebrakes stalking *chichereku* dolls –
amphibious, two-headed,
serrated teeth – who drown children

in frogponds and arroyos, snatching their pure souls
for Kongo master's sorcery.

Silvio's own daughter lies
in a muddy ditch – paralyzed, blind, delirious –
Tamacún pursues the evil spirit
into a patch of weeds, kills the doll
      of ficus wood and cotton braids; Silvio sets it on fire

with kerosene. The girl's fever increases,
jaw locks, bite wounds
suppurate. Silvio tries many cures:
                rum infusion of *okro* seed
                spirit-weed
                decoction, sousumba tea
                tulula-leaf juice
Nothing works.
She begins wheezing, tongue charcoal-black.

                    A man crawls out the red earth
beneath *framboyán*,
limps on a forked cross, loincloth of green
tobacco leaves, thorny vines
creeping down the legs; he's missing a foot,
an arm, the left eye.

        I come from Dahomey
where I heal
the lame, blind, and invalids;
            at Nazareth
I raised Lazarus
from the twice dead. Have faith,
each breath's a miracle.
            He rubs the girl's eyes,
            wounds with saliva.

Rise.

PIEDAD AND HER TONSURED SEAGULLS

Between the Azores and the Lesser
Antilles, purple quays and islets
girded by pin-wheel cara lilies.
A stained glass arboretum
with baobabs and ceibas
whose epiphytes are little hearts
wrapped in shrouds of Manila lace.

Holy Week, when sea air
is saltiest, Piedad dances
with her tonsured seagulls,
lashes of salted cod swinging
from hands gloved with shark's skin,
a palm wimple to protect
the head; they fandango
around abandoned galleons
with names of Caribbean islands.
Carriacou, Cubanacan, Desirada.

To store the fatted birds
she'd built a sand abbey lined with bark-
cloth chasuble, amulets of wormwood
and calendula strewn about;
eggshell turrets, crenels of cowrie,
a Maltese cross for a moat.

Friday night this Andalusian
Jesuit's daughter pulls out a pair
for puppetry, performing Adam and Eve
behind a screen of nun's veiling,
stagelight of Paschal candles.

Easter light and Piedad
twines the leg of the gull
with stigmata on scapulars,
letting it loose to reel,
hover like a wax paper kite,
then plunge into swells
that hasten to the lilied shore,
expiring as pearls of mercury.

Sand of gallstones:
her bare feet imprint flared wings
high tide intaglios,
relics to last till doomsday's
effervescing.

THE STONEBREAKER'S DAUGHTER

after Courbet's *Seashore at Palavas*

A rocky podium. A mannered pose.
And silence. Have the gulls fled to Africa?
This stark seascape is a fitting backdrop
for loneliness. But we're not here
to wallow in your inadequacies.
You seem triumphant, self-congratulatory.
A new conquest, perhaps? I'll call her Juliette.

Turning memory like a kaleidoscope,
you remember Roxana (her breath like anisette)
who burned flowers while making love.
She was moody and suspicious,
a dabbler in still lifes, but you read
her gestures like anagrams. And Isora,
who talked in her sleep – gawky and diffident –
nonetheless marvelous in bed.

You revel in the past,
the surf hints at applause.
You're growing old, with bouts
of impotence wan *demoiselles*
console with pecks and euphemism.

But Juliette, the stonebreaker's
daughter from the Pyrenees,
is very young, Rubenesque, a bit rumpled
and sooty for scuttling coal, who cracks
her knuckles when she yawns. Sundays
you unravel her braid of chestnut

curls, tame the shocks with a horse brush,
declaiming a schoolboy's Ovid in baritone.
"I am *that* nightingale," she says. "The one
with the bloody tongue."

I wade in the sand, grave-
digger's earth, pray
to the driftwood crucifix
as you would hold, kiss
Juliette's dewy hands
on a summer's sally to the Seine.
Afraid of water, woman's silence.
The gulls have flown to Africa.

SADE

1

So luminous in stained glass
or aquarelle, St. Cecilia quavering
the Ave at Sainte Chapelle;
choirs pierce vaulted air,
fluting alleluias. At twelve
I heard her bow *la* viola d'amore,
puff cornetti, finger the virginal.

Atheism excites the young,
old libertines fresco priories
with their tongues: a St. Agatha
or St. Clare, stiff, lamprey-
lipped, pale as death's gladioli.

Divine creatures suffer; God is cold,
self-preoccupied. Strapped to a poison-
wood cross, the outcast hermaphrodite

mewls like Torquemada's cello;
this ambidextrous, two-tongued
cherub – singer of canticles –
copulated with Adam astraddle Eve.

2

I'm old, laughingly fat, impotent.
The bacchanals, their instruments
of pleasure (dais of Carmelite cloth,
cat-o'-nine-tails with nuns' teeth)
are by necessity imagined.

3

At Chareton I rebuilt Sodom
on a ruined Jerusalem.
Eros is artifice; I'm the Master
Sodomite who illuminates
ladskin with bruises, etches ivory
maids. To desecrate *is* to create:
our gift, blessèd Caliban.

PHYSICAL PROPERTIES OF FAITH

Colorless solid or syrup
Insoluble in dogma
Dissolves quickly in ecstasy

Heated to sun's temperature
It yields an amorphous
Substance called *mysterium*

SIGLO DE ORO

Castilla la Vieja: arid foothills,
stone houses, skies between violet
and amethyst. Peasants feud
over arable land, even the old Muslim
cemetery – a fertile incline,
soft, rich as marzipan – suffers the plow
as if Santiago's sword
were disemboweling the infidel.

Across fields of Passion wheat
with gypsy poppies,
farmers stack the uprooted headstones
to build Easter granaries,
their wives plait bones for thatching.

Annus mirabilis – 1571 –
Philip II's galleys defeat the Turks
at Lepanto, his brother Don Juan de Austria
quells the last Moriscos
who had fled to the Alpujarras.
Corpus Christi Thursday,
bell towers – once minarets –
fume ash smelling of bacalao.
(Salt conserves the host best.)

Pigs' feet, blood pudding, chorizos
hang from windows
and niches, anyone abstaining
from pork or taking a bath
is reported to *la Santa Inquisición*.

Old Christian — pure-blooded Visigoth —
an hidalgo scrubs his face
and armpits with egg whites.
"Only marranos wallow in soapy water."
Devout to their catechism,
flies swarm on Santiago's chitterling cincture.

When Christ's body soots the sunflower,
legend says, an *inquisidor*
from Burgos transforms yolks to brooches,
a child's eye to lapus lazuli.

MIDDLE PASSAGE

I. Algeciras

Wharfshrine, Our Lady of Fair Seas:
Agnus Dei's sails caressed by orange-
blossom winds, vestal clouds dust the shore
with snow — *a miracle, coconut flakes!*
a sailor declares just returned from Trinidad,
the boatswain blasphemes, *angels' lice.*

Surrounded by lords, ladies, and lapdogs,
a fat priest blesses the brig on her first voyage
to Africa, wheezing Salve Reginas
as he sprinkles lamb's blood on madonna bowsprit.

Anchors weighed — Angelus —
acolytes fire amulet of nails and medals
off starboard side, Sts. Nicholas
and Phocas on the crew list for good luck.

II. Ouidah

Ash Wednesday, 1825 *Anno Domini.*
Agnus Dei plows uncharted graves of urchin-
footed mariners, stirring sea dregs
with her loadstone anchor.   Chorus

of culverins spews gunpowder litanies;
long boats cast ashore to trade
for *piezas de ebano,* pieces of ebony.

Iron rosaries, scapular collars –
a procession descends stairway
of skulls to the mud chapel where Mass

is said, slaves inspected and bought,
often at the same time,
many temporarily blind, legs and arms

atrophied from being warehoused for months
in a fortress barracoon – hot, fetid, dark –
Agnus Dei's captain bartering in pidgin for best prices:

Cane spirits, pints	100 for 1 slave
Iron bars	30 ” 1 ”
Cloves, pounds	4 ” 1 ”
Rifles (decorated with bronze)	3 ” 1 ”
Whistle with chain	1 ” 1 ”

Hundreds loaded into catacomb holds:
men schackled left leg to right leg, left wrist to right wrist,
heads dunked in salt ponds
for baptism, those suffering from smallpox,
dysentery, gangrene tossed with weights into the swells.

III. Ocean Passage

Your Excellency, the cargo manifest lists 343 bundles to be exact,
including 61 strong bucks aged 15 to 18 to cut cane, which I haggled
down from rifles to whistles with chains. Twin muleques,
who parrot our language beautifully, at just two pounds of Vichy sausage.

Like casks of rum, sick men, pregnant women
thrown overboard to outspeed pursuing
sloops-of-war, the hated *ingleses*, "Protestant Jews,"
that patrol sea lanes enforcing the ban.

At night wood groans, rumbles. *Spirit of talking drum,*
they plead, *why have our gods forsaken us?*
White ghosts will drink our blood
like palm wine, eat our flesh with red yams.

Some jump overboard, others asphyxiate
rolling their own tongues back into the throat;
Yemayá's breath, salty and warm,
blows them home like clouds of okra dust.

IV. La Habana

Portside barracoon, Africans' wounds
caulked with tar, bodies varnished with lard
for the auction, branding iron christening
them Lucas Yolof, José Mandinga, Luz Angola, etc.

An American winces when a Cuban planter
tests a slave's health licking the sweat
on his chin, two priests rub women's teeth
with pumice stones, sniff for parasites.

Habana's bishop thanks San José the Redeemed
who safeguarded the live cargo (*just one fifth*
lost to the sea), burning sulfur hosts in gold ampulla.
The Africans are corralled into schooners

that will freight them to sugar estates;
His Majesty's soldiers limp up the gangplank,
ship bound for Spain, another failed campaign
against maroons whose wooden arms maim

like steel, wounds festering into gangrene
from points, darts smeared with excrement.
Cathedral bell tolls. Yoruba blacksmith
hears Ogún's war cries in clanging metal.

Our gods are with us. These ghosts smell
of prey. I will be the lion that hunts
the gazelle. The slave clenches his chain,
feels for the first time the sharp point of revenge.

III. CALIBAN CIMARRÓN

AN ISLAND CALLED WEWEE

I was christened Neptune des Caraïbes
on the fifth Thermidor, Year II,
with rancid wine and a mule's kick
to my starboard side. Made to wear
the red cockade, bear a shrine
of Guillotine on Bastille Day, my master
a Jacobin smuggler of tobacco
and precious stones, sure that I, a small sailboat,
would not arouse suspicion. To stop me
from riding high tide to freedom
he'd drag me into a narrow backwater corral,
knotting my leash around a dead tree
with fishbone twigs and scaly bark, used by slaves
for nailing *wanga* – magic charms.
He was soon betrayed, a possee of English
brigantines pursued us in choppy seas,
I gasping as my bow plunged over
and over into the swells, listing and taking
in much water, terrified too
of being gunned down. I keeled over near
Saba's coastline, a coffin for my master.
I was sold to a black fisherman
from Martinique, kind and decent, who sings
me shanties that ward off tempests, balms my scrapes
with coconut fat, keeps my insides free
of rat-lure fishparts, though his daughter, sneaking at night,
snips off my sailcloth to make patches
for her brother's workclothes, telling her father
it's the magic dolls that are eating me up.
But if the fish die, as they did in The Red Flood,

will my master scuttle me as worthless
or, worse, tear me apart to sell as firewood?
Masters say, "Without soul boats have no claim
to heaven," yet Carib *kanawa* – dugouts – tell stories
of an island called Wewee where the gods return
boats to their original state as hardwood trees.

MADRID, 1938

Para ir al infierno no hace falta cambiar de sitio ni postura
Rafael Alberti

1

Charon's old truck growls and belches, crosses
Philip II's bridge, transporting dead
loyalist soldiers – peasants, workers, students –
to the Valley of Manzanares
where Trotskyite Amazons, POUM militia,
inter them alongside bones
and gods of *íberos*, pre-Roman Iberians.

1938, two years since Spanish Legionnaires,
Moroccans and CTV Black Shirts
began laying the siege, *madrileños* have consumed
every zoo animal, dray horse,
alley cat, gypsy goat they could butcher
in-between bombardments,
65/17 mm artillery.
Aristocratic cannibals barter
at the morgue for organs and glands
to roast over kindled
Louis Seize legs and arms, Cuban mahogany.

2

Tall, gaunt yet muscular – the flame made flesh –
as if El Greco had painted
him onto the Twentieth Century,
the anarchist angel paints in blood the CNT/

FAI tetragram – a circled A –
on churchstones gouged by a mob's bullets and picks.

Confessionals confiscated as sentry boxes,
the sacristy an arsenal
of Soviet 7.62 mm machine guns.

"It's the spontaneous flow of rage,"
the angel says, "that liberates one's instinct."
Smokes two cigarettes, lips tremble.
A grenade thrower in Durruti's Column,
his leg was wounded at the Battle
of the Ebro, between Bot and Prat de Compte.

"Raw emotion purifies, reason corrupts.
The passion for destruction
is creative, more so than any art
form. Bakunin, Kropotkin
and Malatesta are my apostles, chaos
their perfection. Within myself
is an immanence greater than any god's."

3

Orphaned angels – libertarian FIJL youths –
eat bread hard as stone, drink distilled cinders,
hiding in verminous metro tunnels
from Condor Legion bombers – Heinkel 111s –
that drop Thermit incendiaries,
2,000 lb high explosives in finger-four formation.

Bathed in morning light – acid olive green –
the angels huddle

beneath an oculus, bomb crater,
delousing one another's glass-wool hair.
Once an apprentice
to Cardinal's portraitist, Ariel sketches
on their vellum backskins –
his own belly too by way of mirror –
charcoal miniatures, Goyaesque capriccios,
depicting modern war
that expand during sleep, as by metastasis,
into indelible *apocalypsis*.

Ariel peddles his belly
wherever tunnels take him – Gran Vía,
Puerta del Sol, Atocha, Fuencarral, Opera –
charging passersby 10 or 20 centimos
to see, touch levitating falangists –
FET/JONS Blue Shirts – who play death's trombone
and helicon, eyes shooting flames,
five antichrists who soar with Stuka wings
spitting out TNT pomegranates
on civilians, claws and teeth of tempered steel.

Across the closed Prado Museum
a dozen International Brigaders
circle Ariel, some gawk, others clap and blaspheme.
A jumble of change, whole pesetas even.

Incognito as Commissar
of the SIM political police,
an *inquisidor* pushes his way through
the soldiers, kidnapping Ariel,
etherized unconscious. Administers purgatives,
sudorifics, liniments of acetone

and benzene, fortified with holy oil;
the icon remains intact,
indicating its miraculous cause.
Releases the orphaned angel who staggers
back to the tunnels, INRI branded
on scruff, buttocks, forearms;
a triangle cut for Christ's loincloth.

An old Mother Superior selling black-market
cigarettes, Cuban sugar
at Plaza del Ángel pulls Ariel
from a pile of debris, where he has collapsed.
Snuggling him in her lap's manger, she blows smoke
until he coughs, snorts, her breast suckles
as if this bombed-out city were Bethlehem.

BONE AND BLOOD

Genuflection, a white spasm,
   a black certitude –
the saints know their entrails
   are the blood-soaked rosaries
they hang to dry on bone
   footboards, scrimshawed
with emery nails – a chain
   of little boats in furling water,
dolled up with ribboned crosses,
   rudders, wishbones, pomegranates
that string a bonnet sun, pin a lumpy moon.

Bone and blood rivet
   like earth at river's edge,
and in anodyne dreams of singed
   bushes, amputees, the land's
a racked quilt of hides,
   whose hairs thistly children
graze among reliquaries. Windmills
   with font cogs and crucifix blades
work jawlike harpsichords, anviling
   martyred canticles.

Alluvial harmonies
   sediment childhood memories,
concordances to their calling:
   the bedside candles,
sentinels; ashy brooms,
   angel wings; mother's footsteps,
the censer swaying;

nail clippings, prayers
unanswered; boiling water,
a cloud in Heaven.

IRONMAN'S SONG

Oshún's *chekeré*-gourd is mountain rain
swelling rivers to overflowing
as beads of molten silver patter the kettle
that is my belly – pimply, brittle,

ringworm rust. These arrowheads
covered in dross-mud once touched
Oshún's anvil breasts, scarified face.
When flesh dressed my bones,

I wore Obatalá's white tunic
and like him lived chastely, ate no meat.
Derived joy from my work as blacksmith
to the mountain's *orishas*.

Forged their ceremonial weapons,
dancewands. As I was picking firewood
one day, beautiful Oshún slunk
out of cattails by river's edge,

snaring me with her golden mesh,
smearing *oñí*, honey, on my lips. I felt lust
for the first time. Smoke of evening,
we made love atop night's embers –

she the furnace, I the ore. Her husband
Shangó stormed upon us, his thunder quaked
the earth, uprooting the baobab tree;
eyes sparked, discharging lightning

that smelted my body, and I was left
by this old adabo ficus to rust into oblivion.
Farmers sharpened my scapulas
to plow fields of manioc and cocoyam,

soldiers filed leg bones into assagai,
priests ground teeth for augury,
my vertebrae – once lithesome for dancing –
a slagstone heap. Father Obatalá,

lead Oshún to me, may her hands touch me again
in warm fires as I simmer dried river
fish with chilies, sweet corn and cocoyams,
cinnamon potions and yesterday's palmnut soup.

AGUA DE COCO

Cantor in shul, bolero singer
at the Asturian Center,
a voice that flutters any *shikse*'s heart,
so good a dancer he can rumba
with bricks tied to his shoes.

Like his Polish father Osher,
Moisés sells jewelry to habaneros
and Ashkenazim: the evil-eye jetstone,
inlaid mezuza, golden Lady
of Charity, silver Mogen David.

Lifting verses from Solomon's Song,
he inserts bittersweet fruits,
eight o' clock jasmine, milk-and-wine lily
to charm tropical shulammites,
stiletto heels clicking on cobblestones. Sunset,

the Shabbat beginning, Moisés turns the corner
at Jesús María, nearly trips avoiding
a fat boy, half naked, who hurls grenades –
moldy papaya – on three older ones,
breathes flank steak frying in lard. A tall mulatta

with straight hair, jetblack, waits in her blue
courtyard drinking *agua de coco* –
golden-husked Jamaica – her yellow beads
and crepe headdress reveal
she belongs to Oshún whose song floats

between prayer and desire. "Your hair's like shavings
of mahogany," the mulatta says,
"your eyelashes *zunzún* feathers." (God Bird,
Cuban Emerald.) Moisés blushes.
"When I saw your eyes," she says, "the saint

rose to my head; this morning the shells
foretold I'd meet you; I prefer
foreign men, so beautiful, so mysterious.
Are you thirsty?" She puts the paper straw
to his lips, Moisés drinks the warm,
slightly fermented liquid. "*Gracias corazón.*"

They lie in bed smoking Chesterfields,
her large beeswax candle casts
a tremulous shadow
on Oshún's plastic shrine, seeds like songbird
beaks floating on holy water,

green pennies sunk in the glass, her walls peeled
like sunburnt skin. The shulammite sings
"Lagrimas Negras" (Black Tears); he playfully
falsettoes the refrain: "I'll go with you –
my saint – even if it causes my death."

She pulls his soft penis
like a rubber band, tickling with her tongue,
Moisés laughs loudly, throat hot
and scratchy as if he'd swigged cane alcohol.

They make love again, this time she's on top.
Moisés tastes banana nectar
in her sweat, hears bolero's clarinet.
The old kapok mattress sinks to the floor.

ANTOJITOS

Are Mary's fingers edible:
quimbombó with red-pepper
tips? Sautéed in olive oil and garlic
might they aromatize
into aphrodisiac? Do angels
gossip – so and so
is bald, wears a periwig –
their naughty voices like marimbas?

IROKO

Henequen habits, rawhide brogans drying
on tackle lines, twelve nuns sleep
in nets that snare squid, amberjack,
barracuda; bilge and sweat
mingle in their barracoon. By cold light
of wicker lanterns — *cocuyo* fireflies —
insomniacs whittle hoestick Marias.

Erekusu's Carmelites inhabit the ruins
of Gethsemane sugar mill. Before sunrise
Prioress Aurea ascends the watchtower
to sound the Ave, nine conch-shell blows;
work gangs hymn the Mater Dolorosa
marching on canefields gone wild to cultivate

yuca, beans, yams, okra. Engraved limestones,
stations of the cross, girdle Iroko
Arabá, ceiba that shelters Madonna
and child. Planters' daughters take their vows
offering flan and callaloo
to Iroko, Sor Aurea béjewels night-blooming
flowers with phials of coconut water.

Feast of Her Assumption: lambent skies
overcast to sulfur, thunderclouds
pour acetic wine. The graveyard floods
erupting with bones of Kongo slaves,
which the convent's curandera
gathers for making oils, poultices,

infusions. Nine nuns pull hogsheads heavy with rain,
a quintet performs on kettle, cowbell

and hoesticks. Novices – all shades –
rumba atop the stones
imitating cane cutters: some slash at the root
clutching the sharp stalks,
others scratch, dig, and sow next season's crop.
Braids flail, anklets rattle
when tempo rises, cutters swirling
as *la Virgen* rides their heads. Sor Aurea

guzzles – between hiccups – "Gracious Mater,
Yayá-Yeyé, Dulcis Parens Clementiae,
guard us from the foe, yembé awan,
glorious anima, ayere sangiereré."

BITTER ALGAE

You have hedged me behind and before, and laid Your hand upon me

Ps 139:5

Calvinist guerrillas wage holy war
ambushing Spaniards, plundering silver
ciboria and ivory ampullae
Sephardic exiles sell to Ottoman
pashas in Levantine ports.

Conceiving himself an Israelite,
Commander Joshua van Roosendaal –
selfcircumcised – wears tefillin
as he rides into battle,
shofars blowing. Yoked oxen
transport the ark across Brabantine moors

and heather, Zeeland's peat bogs,
the Young Dunes and cold mud
of Holland's seashore. Bullskins
canopy the holy of holies,
incense altars swinging from flesh hooks.

Duke of Alva's troops sack Naarden, Zutphen,
Mechelen. Joshua incites
Zeelanders to rebellion, peat dredgers
hang Dominican friars

with their own cinctures. The drunk men
pass around a porcelain font
like King Carnival's chamberpot,
Mad Meg slips a *pekelharing*
between St. Ursula's breasts.

Pede Sainte Anne bonfires
an effigy of His Most Catholic Monarch
King Philip II – dressed as Pope –
on the peat knoll Luttel Calvarieberg.

Alva's Blood Council retaliates
ordering the village be cleansed
of heresy; horsemen armed with pikes
massacre infants and their mothers,
magpies swooping from scorched gallows.

Joshua paints a calfblood seal
of Solomon, recites *kadish yatom*
for the innocents, seven synonyms
to exalt Adoshem.

The ark sheds its skin,
roses of Jericho
flare seven petals in the mire.
YaHVeH's Carib angel touches
his green eyes with live mangrove

charcoal and Joshua dreams squalls
that hail rock candy on green
windward islands, turbulent waves
frothing muscovado. At dusk

young iguanas skulk
through glorybowers hunting moths
with tobacco wings,
purple-throated colibri
nest on rose-cups of menorah
cacti. Joshua climbs
coral steps to a copse of mahoes

and Jerusalem thorns
where maroons, marranos, Huguenots
pile the unhewn coral,
altar of the wilderness. Joshua slaughters
a wild goat. The circumcised share
with the uncircumcised
manioc cakes, boiled meat, bitter algae.

CALIBAN CIMARRÓN

Caliban escapes the tyranny of Prospero, canoes westward
three days and nights to Cubanacán, island of *cimarrones*
who build indigo-wood fortresses in the high peaks of cloud
forests; the ancestral spirits of Ilé-Ifé accompany them in
the shape of trees and springs. Shangó is the *cimarrones'*
protector – *orisha* of fire, thunder, war. Initiated into his
mysteries, Caliban becomes the high priest, a *babalosha*.

Shangó,
I hear your heart when an Oyo warrior beats
the *iyá* drum, my scarred back tattooed

with your double-ax that cleaves
the sky hurling lightning-fire on sugar mills;
your plantain Oguedé

ignites without consumption,
signaling victory. When very ripe
its fruit causes visions of Africa.

My wife Ayorinde of Yobú plays
the *don-don* drums praising your many names,
I place beneath Oguedé

fufú – mashed – plantain and cassava bread,
eggs fried in turtle fat, okra stew, gunpowder.
The color of smoked tamarind,

Ayorinde's face glows in the sun
as she condiments your morning meal,
scattering purple basil and cumin seeds.

Shangó Kora, Shangó Oba Funké,
Shangó Aguá Guayé. Your kingdom
will one day spread across

the Greater and Lesser Antilles:
master and slave will dance
to the three *bata* drums.

NOTES

"Dido's Lament"

Guajirito is the diminutive form of *guajiro*, the name given to Cuba's white peasant, although the term today can also include blacks and mulattoes. During colonial times, *guajiros*, mostly descendants of Canary islanders, were subsistence farmers, sometimes hired as slave catchers. They lived in *bohíos*, thatched huts, that their ancestors had learned to build from the Taíno Indians. They played a folk music called *punto guajiro* with string instruments and maracas. Esteban Montejo, the protagonist in Miguel Barnet's *Biography of a Runaway Slave*, states that *guajiros* were adamant about not playing the drum or having anything to do with things African.

"AfroCuba"

Mi patria es dulce por afuera, y muy amarga por dentro
"My homeland is sweet on the outside and very bitter on the inside." From Nicolás Guillén's poem "Mi patria es dulce por fuera . . . ." The term AfroCuba was coined by the great Cuban ethnographer Fernando Ortiz.

"Crib of Reeds"

Mackandal was an African-born Haitian rebel of the eighteenth century, leader of a conspiracy by maroons to poison the whites' water, then set fire to their plantations and thus start a general uprising of the slaves. Before he could carry out the plan, he was captured by French soldiers and burned at the stake. Slaves who witnessed the execution claimed they saw Mackandal free himself from the ropes and leap over the flames. This belief in his immortality endured for generations.

"Poem Written for the Feast of Our Lady of Charity"

La Virgen de la Caridad del Cobre, or Our Lady of Charity of Cobre, is Cuba's patron saint. A shrine was built in her honor in the town of Cobre where, according to the tradition, she appeared to three salters. As the men were crossing the Bay of Nipe to make salt, a fierce a storm developed. They prayed to the Virgin Mary, and she appeared miraculously, saving their lives.

Bendita tú eres entre todas las mujeres: Holy art thou amongst women (from the Hail Mary). *Luz pura*: pure light. A term variously defined and interpreted by Jews, the Shekinah is, to my gentile mind, the presence of the Divine Feminine on earth.

"Women of Guaraguasi"
A goddess of my own invention, Chola Kalunga combines the personalities and attributes of Oshún and Yemayá. Her name is a hybrid of the Kongo equivalents for these *orishas*: Chola Wengue (Oshún) and Ma Kalunga (Yemayá).

"Isabel Kongo"
Malemuka and Kumbembé are Kongo names for magical creatures that inhabit the wilderness. For black Cubans the natural world is sacred, the place where their African ancestors and spirits dwell. The poem ends with a prayer syncretizing the Catholic *Dies Irae* with *mambos*, or chants, from *palo mayombe*, a magical religion originally practiced by slaves brought from Angola and other parts of Kongo-speaking Africa.

"An Island Called Wewee"
The date, Fifth Thermidor, Year II, belongs to the French Revolutionary calendar, adopted in 1793. The names of the months are quite poetic. Thermidor, the eleventh (July 19-August 17), means "heat." Year II is 1794.

"Siglo de Oro" (Golden Age)
Santiago, or Santiago Matamoros (the Moor slayer), is Saint James the Great, military patron saint of Spain and defender of Christianity against the Moors, hence the appellation Matamoros. At the Cathedral of Santiago de Compostela there is a statue of the saint in the heat of battle, slaughtering terrified Muslim soldiers. According to legend, Santiago miraculously appeared at the Battle of Covadonga

(718), riding a white horse and wielding a luminous sword. By his inspiration Pelayo's troops were able to defeat the Moor Alcama's army, thus marking the start of the Reconquista (Reconquest), which lasted almost 800 years.

"Middle Passage"
The source of the bartering list is *Los negros esclavos* by Fernando Ortiz.

"Madrid, 1938"
Para ir al infierno no hace falta cambiar de sitio ni postura
"It is not necessary to change one's place or one's posture to go to Hell." From Rafael Alberti's poem "Muerte y juicio" (Death and Judgment).

"Iroko"
"Gracious Mater, Yayá-Yeyé, Dulcis Parens Clementiae, guard us from the foe, yembé awan, glorious anima, ayere sanguereré." Another syncretic prayer. This one combines the Ave Maria (in Latin and English) with Kongo *mambos*.

"Caliban *Cimarrón*"
Shangó Kora, Shangó Oba Funké, Shangó Aguá Guayé. These are ritual titles meant to give praise to the *orisha*.

Adoshem   (Hebrew) variant of Adonai, or The Lord

Agayú   (Lucumí) Agayú Solá, an *orisha* who represents strength and fatherhood, believed to be the father of Shangó. He is identified with Saint Christopher.

agua de coco   (Spanish) coconut water

aguardiente   (Spanish) sugar cane liquor, literally "burning water"

Angunga   Kongo nation. The mark, or *trazo*, possesses magical powers.

ashé   (Lucumí) creative force of the universe in santería, originating from Olodumare

babalosha   (Lucumí) male priest of a specific *orisha*. The female is called *iyalosha*.

bacalao   (Spanish) codfish, either fresh or salted

batá   the three cylindrical drums used in Lucumí ritual music: the *iyá*, or master drum, which has bells strung around the heads; the smaller *itótele*, which follows the pattern of the first; and the *okónkolo*, the smallest, used for ostintato playing.

bozal   creolized Spanish spoken by slaves

brujero   (Cuban Spanish) sorcerer in the AfroCuban religion *palo mayombe*

CNT   Confederación Nacional de Trabajadores (National Confederation of Workers)

CTV   (Italian) Corpo Truppe Volontaire (Corps of Volunteer Troops)

cabrón   (Spanish) literally the male goat, but used colloquially as "bastard"

caguama   (Spanish) loggerhead turtle

caimán   (Spanish) cayman

callaloo   *calalú* in Spanish. AfroCuban dish of spinach or other greens cooked in a spicy sauce of coconut milk.

Caná-Caná   (Lucumí) the turkey buzzard in the magical folklore of AfroCubans

caracol   (Spanish) conch

Castilla la Vieja   Old Castile, a region in Spain

cerveza   (Spanish) beer

Chareton   insane asylum where the Marquis de Sade spent the remaining years of his life

chekeré   (Lucumí) percussive instrument made from a round gourd covered with netting and beads

chicha   (Quechua) South American beverage made from fermented maize

chicherekú   (Kongo) wooden doll that a sorcerer animates with the soul of someone dead; it is used either for harming an enemy or for self-protection.

cimarrón   (Spanish) maroon or runaway slave

compadre   (Spanish) godfather of one's child, used colloquially as "buddy"

Cubanacán   indigenous name of Cuba

curandero   (Spanish) folk healer

danzón   Cuba's national dance, derived from the *contradanza* (contredanse) of the nineteenth century

décima   classic Spanish stanza form consisting of ten octosyllabic lines rhyming abbaaccddc

Elohim   (Hebrew) God

Eshu   (Lucumí) Eshu Eleguá, *orisha* who opens the path for other *orishas*; guardian of thresholds, ways, and crossroads; also a trickster and messenger of Olofi. His Catholic equivalents are Saint Anthony of Padua, the Christ Child of Atocha, the *Anima Sola* (Soul in Purgatory), and Saint Martin of Porres.

FAI   Federación Anarquista Ibérica (Iberian Anarchist Federation)

FET   Falange Española Tradicional (Traditional Spanish Falange)

FIJL   Federación Ibérica de Juventudes Libertarias (Iberian Federation of Libertarian Youths)

fufú   food of West African origin

garrotero   (Spanish) executioner who turns the *garrote vil*, a metal collar (supported by a post) used to strangle the victim

Gracias corazón   (Spanish) idiomatic expression for "Thank you, sweetie"

guaguancó   rumba with strong rhythmic movements, erotic in nature

habaneros   (Spanish) inhabitants of Havana

Ilé-Ifé   spiritual center of the Yoruba people, and the place of creation

inquisidor   (Spanish) inquisitor

Iroko Arabá   (Lucumí) *orisha* of the ceiba, or silk cotton tree

iyá   (Lucumí) the master drum of the *batá*

JONS   Juntas de Ofensiva Nacional-Sindicalista (National-Sindicalist Offensive Movement)

jutía   hutia in English. A tree-dwelling rodent with a prehensile tail, indigenous to the Caribbean.

kadish yatom   Jewish mourner's prayer

kalenda   also *calenda*. An erotic AfroCaribbean dance, or rhythm, popular in the seventeenth and eighteenth centuries.

lavandera   (Spanish) washerwoman

Lucumí   AfroCubans of Yoruba origin, their ritual language and their culture. The name derives from the Yoruba greeting *oluku mi*, "my friend."

majá   Cuban boa, the largest snake in the Greater Antilles

madrileños   (Spanish) inhabitants of Madrid

malanga   starchy tuber eaten in tropical America, also known as yautía

mayito   (Cuban Spanish) red-winged blackbird

mi cielo, mi gloria   (Spanish) words of endearment, literally "my sky, my glory"

Mogen David   (Hebrew) Star of David

mohel   (Yiddish) man who performs ritual circumcision

Moriscos   (Spanish) Moors in Spain forced to convert to Christianity

muleque   (Cuban Spanish) name given to slave girls born in Africa

Nkuyu Nfinda   Kongo name of Eleguá

Obatalá   (Lucumí) *orisha* of purity and justice, creator of humankind, identified with Nuestra Señora de las Mercedes, Our Lady of Mercy

Oguedé   (Lucumí) the plantain, but also the spirit that lives within it

Ogún   (Lucumí) *orisha* of iron, identified with Santiago de Compostela

Olofi   (Lucumí) *orisha* who created the world, but without providential powers. His Christian equivalent is the Eternal Father, and also the Holy Spirit.

Oriente   eastern region of Cuba

orisha   (Lucumí) god or goddess of santería, informally called saints

Orúnmila   (Lucumí) also known as Orula and Ifá. *Orisha* of wisdom and divination, identified with Saint Francis of Assisi.

Osaín   (Lucumí) *orisha* of vegetation and medicinal herbs, identified with Saints Sylvester, Anthony Abad, and Raymond the Unborn.

Oshún   (Lucumí) *orisha* of the river and eros, identified with Cuba's patron saint, La Virgen de la Caridad, Our Lady of Charity.

Oyo   powerful Yoruba kingdom, birthplace of Shangó

POUM   Partido Obrero de Unificación Marxista (United Marxist Workers Party)

pecado   (Spanish) sin

pekelharing   (Dutch) pickled herring

pescado   (Spanish) fish

querubín   (Spanish) cherub

quimbombó   name for okra in Cuba. A word of West African origin.

ron añejo   (Spanish) aged rum

rumba yambú   rumba that lacks the eroticism of the *guaguancó*. Dancers move slowly, their gestures mimicking old age.

SIM   Servicio de Investigación Militar (Military Investigation Service)

saco de carbón   (Spanish) racist expression used to disparage AfroCubans since colonial times.   Slavers also referred to their human cargo as *bultos* (bundles).

Santa Inquisición   (Spanish) Holy Inquisition

santería   (Spanish) "the way of the saints." AfroCuban religion of Yoruba origin in which the *orishas* (gods and goddesses) are syncretized with Catholic saints.

Shangó   (Lucumí) *orisha* of fire, thunder, lightning, and war, identified with Saint Barbara

shikse   (Yiddish) gentile girl

shmates   (Yiddish) shabby goods

shoykhet   (Yiddish) a slaughterer of animals and fowl according to Jewish ritual

son   also *son montuno*. Popular musical form that combines Iberian and African elements. This mixing of musical traditions is characteristically Cuban.

tambores   (Spanish) drums

Tevet   fourth month in the Jewish calendar, 29 days long

wanga   Vodou charms or spells

Yemayá   (Lucumí) *orisha* of the sea and maternity, identified with La Virgen de Regla, Our Lady of Regla, a municipality of Havana with a considerable population of *santeros*

Yobú   Yoruba kingdom

yuca   (Taíno) cassava root, indigenous to the Caribbean

Yumurí   river in Cuba's Matanzas province

zunzún   echoic name of the common hummingbird of Cuba

zunzuncito   bee hummingbird. The male is the smallest bird in the world.